'benni' Publishing.

THE HOLY CAT
of Khozouvictissa

ACKNOWLEDGEMENTS

CREDO PUBLISHING, LIBRA, DOWNLANDER
CARAPACE, CAT WORLD.

COVER
Architectural design: Ben Gorton
Cats: Pam Chandley, I.S. Benner
Overall design: I.S. Benner

THE HOLY CAT

OF KHOZOUVICTISSA

BY FINOLA HOLIDAY

A collection of poems about cats.

'*benni*' Publishing.
England

© Finola Holiday *1998*

All rights reserved. No part of this book may be reproduced, stored in a retrieval system or transmitted in any form or by any means, electronic or mechanical, photocopying, recording or otherwise, without the permission of the publisher.
First edition 1998
Published by *'benni' Publishing,* Phoenix House, 47 Richmond Road, Worthing, West Sussex BN11 4AF UK
Tel: 01903 212 872 e-mail Benni@btinternet.com

Printed by:
Express Letterheads Ltd., Hove, East Sussex BN3 3YL UK

BRITISH LIBRARY CATALOGUE DATA
Holiday, Finola Garner
The Holy Cat of Khozouvictissa
Poems
1 Title

ISBN 0 9533985 0 1

 *'to arrange a cat upon a chair'*

Finola Holiday spent many years of her life in Africa, where, in addition to writing poetry, she helped to take care of some of the bigger cats in Kenya.
These were the runts of the litters of lions who were not strong enough to move out with their mothers at the start of the rains and who therefore risked becoming the victims of Masai spears.
In the Sahara Desert, in the forecourt of a mud palace in the old kingdom of Aïr, she sometimes entertained a girl cheetah.
In 1983 she returned to a more mundane life in England and applied herself to the serious craft of poetry writing - but poets must have their fun too and to write verse about the lesser felines of the species brought the reward of a warm response from friends and fellow poets.
She decided to collect her cat poems and offer them up - although - *'to arrange a cat upon a chair'* - is a tricky task indeed.

CONTENTS

page

       Introduction.
- 5   Haiku
- 6   Nocturne for a Witch.
- 7   Grimalkin.
- 8   Black Cat.
- 9   Proposition to a Young Witch, Companionless, on All Souls' Night.
- 10 Mephistolina.
- 11 A Farm Cat remembers.
- 12 At the Cat Show.
- 13 My Polite Cat.
- 14 On Hearing that The Siamese Cat First Appeared in England About 1898.
- 16 Siamese Sage.
- 17 The Siamese Cat of the Monastery Contemplates` His Death and Reincarnation.
- 18 The Winter Coat.
- 19 On the Death of a Blue-Point Siamese.
- 20 Festival of Lights.
- 22 The Holy Cat of Khozouvictissa.
- 23 The Siamese on Patmos.
- 24 Cat Out of Context.
- 25 The Cats of Kos.
- 26 The Cat of the Wanli Vase.
- 27 Their Sadnesses.
- 28 The Siamese Cat Tries Unsuccessfully to Change the Course of History.

page	
29	Emigrants from Siam.
30	The Immigrant Persians.
32	The Emigration of Egyptian Cats to Britain.
33	The Dorset Tom.
34	The Moggies.
36	The Cat Outside.
37	The Richest Cat in the World.
38	Cats in History.
39	Lines for Tigger.
40	My Post Modern Cat.
41	Astrocats.
42	The Cats of Butleigh.
44	The Cat of Candle Land.
46	Karim.
47	On Kitchener Island.
48	At the Necropolis of Mummified Cats.
49	Musical Cats.
50	The Revenants.
51	The Cat of the Titanic.
52	The Cats Deplore the Loss of their Proper Place in the Scriptures.
54	Last Words to a Siamese.
55	Breach of Security.
56	Cruelty to Animals.
57	A Supplication.
58	Haiku.

INTRODUCTION

Cats and poetry have an almost magical affinity. Cat - presences can beguile the senses as do the echoes of rhyme. They can move out of reach quite as subtly as the perfect phrase - just as you think you have both within your grasp. In these pages I have endeavoured to turn a few cats into poems and pin them down briefly in print.

This book is dedicated to the cats I have known, to my cat - family and cat - friends of town and country and to those strangers and foreigners with whom any acquaintance can only be passing, offering no more than a glimpse of a shadow moving, as spirits move, through the moonlit nights of memory.

We humans are privileged to have such creatures living along the boundaries of our world - supposedly belonging to it yet not entirely part of it.

Those pieces of rough - and - tumble fur that have cats inside, the cat - corps - de - ballet that can suddenly materialise on the lawn, that curled up cushion on the sofa with the faux-fur pattern - all can make us laugh and give us a little comfort as long as we remember that they are our honoured guests and can never be counted among our possessions.

Finola Holiday

The cat on the moon
pursues a brace of moon-mice
across the green cheese

NOCTURNE FOR A WITCH

Woman lying alone
in a cold room
the window ajar
letting in winter -
the snow moon
the tinsel star.

Woman lying alone
in a double bed
deep under the down
your body naked
your pillowed head
invisibly brown.

Beyond your window
the dark congeals
into soft shapes.
A passing shadow
substantiates
and steals inside.

In catskin guise
your familiar
comes to your quilt.
Under the witch-wise
night you share
a coat of wild silk.

GRIMALKIN

I am black, I am the shadow
of wickedness on earth,
I am furred with the night, beware
if you cross my path.
The flame of a black candle
still gleams in my eyes,
I have sat by a witch's fire
through a span of lives.

I belong to the past, I am part
of the greenwood, the sacred broom,
on a page of the Book of Shadows
I am named the familiar
of a Mistress of Magic, by night
I ride rowan and willow
high over bracken and briar
at the dark of the moon.

I was there at the Black Mass,
a spirit in catskin guise
I crouched by the wildwood altar
on the eve of Hallowmas.
There is glamour in my green eyes
and where my shadow goes
the candles dip and falter
though no wind blows.

I am talisman, amulet,
a ward against evil,
an image you wear at your neck
older than the cross -
but put off my witch-wise charm,
mock me, suffer my loss
and your life is a waning candle -
as wax before flame.

BLACK CAT

Black cat of Connemara
your golden eyes
window another world
as images in amber
survive from the deep past
before we were.

You lived in the land
before the Celts
came out of the west
with their burden of legends,
before the hermit saints
raised a stone cross
and cursed your kin
you belonged to their darkness,
your incadescent eyes,
your Satan skin.

You will still be here
in the time of the withering sun
squatting beside the sill
of a dead door
when we are gone.

PROPOSITION TO A YOUNG WITCH, COMPANIONLESS, ON ALL SOULS' NIGHT

"Though you can call up the dead,
Mistress, when the veil is torn
you seem to lack a catskin worn
for warmth and for luck.
With fur as black as your tall hat
my coat, like a warm cloak
covers my back.

I am an itinerant fellow
with slanted eyes
that are sometimes red -
sometimes the golden yellow
mirrors of moonrise.
I know your eyes are always green
I know the wind has streamed your hair
but I will be your go-between
and your familiar.
I will be your coven cat
but caveat, caveat,
I must go at Candlemas
from your caress.

But I will go with you this night
on your wild sky-ride,
while the spirits of those who have died
are all round about.
I will sit in silhouette
on the back of your rowan broom
as we fly, witch and cat,
across the moon".

# MEPHISTOPHELINA

Mephistophelina
has nothing between her
ears except black fur.
We are not altogether sure
if she is a her.

Those pointed ears
of the Devil's kind -
tell us her mother
rode pillion behind
a Dorset witch
on a withy broom
over field and ditch
by the light of the moon.

They tell us her father
was black as sin
with a roving nature
and a Cheshire grin
Before he left
at the peep of day
the witch's cat
was rolled in the hay.

Mephistophelina
has eyes of lavender
and an ecstatic purr -
We shall very soon discover
if she is a her.

 FARM CAT REMEMBERS.

I can remember
the gooseberry bush
I was born under.
It was prickly green
and the sun's golden eyes
looked through the leaves.
Sometimes the spikes of rain
struck through my kitten-coat
like kitchen knives.
When we all opened our eyes
our mother took us away
to the back of the cider-press -
it was warm and dry
with the smell of dead apples
and musty spice.
Under the tallest vat
a nest of nursling mice
wriggled and squeaked
and our cat-clever mother
saved them till they were fat
and good to eat.

AT THE CAT SHOW

Behind the bars,
under the neon suns
on ideal under-blankets
of loving wool
they laze and roll.

Confabulating ladies
in clinical white coats
examine ear and paw -
configure clip-board notes
with anxious care.

But do they understand
their idols have come
down many generations -
from temple and jungle
from New World woods in autumn,
from beyond the ice-falls
of nameless mountains?

These objects of desire
my hands crave for -
my fingers long to touch
the silk fur.

If only there could be
a slight disaster -
a fainting lady,
a power failure
so I could slip a bolt
and smuggle out just one
in my cat-burglar coat -
leaving a cage empty,
a spirit gone.

# My Polite Cat

My polite cat
jumped on to my rug
when I was lying up
with a virus bug.

She came to visit me
with purr-humming
sleep-shamming
duplicity.

Meantime, a ream of A4
was sitting on the desk
in an open drawer
when suddenly

I saw the papers part
and a young poem
the size of my thumb
came wriggling out.

My polite cat
was wide awake.
There came a leap
and a snap.

She bit it hard
right on a noun...
and the poor little words
hung down.

When I get better
I will wrap it in newspaper
and that will be 'amen'
for a dead poem.

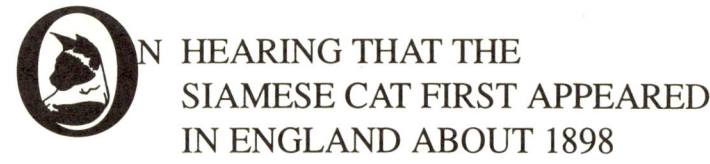N HEARING THAT THE SIAMESE CAT FIRST APPEARED IN ENGLAND ABOUT 1898

Four hundred generations
away
- to almost the day -
you, the first boat-person
crossed the Thai border,
came over the Silk Road
from Cathay:
riding a palanquin
with the favourite daughter
of a mandarin.

When you ran away
she was in tears
headstrong girl:
had her slaves lashed
servants whipped -
coolies in flat hats
searched ships
but to no avail -

You were under a bale
of spices
stowing away
then creeping on deck
and into the hold
of the river boat
to survive shipwreck
the killing cold
and a shortage of rats.

Since then you have never
looked back
or been integrated
but remain
the smooth ivory Oriental -
unchanging stranger.

We have put wind-chimes
under the elms
to make you at home
and the white prayer flags
flutter from bean rows -
even our scarecrows
wear saffron rags.

This garden door
opens on jungle. There
beyond your oblique
blue stare
tree snakes do rope tricks,
mantises pray -
Idolatrous gods
moulder away
on our lawn.

In our raspberry canes
tigers have lain
in wait for you
while the green rods
of the rain
fall through bamboo.

SIAMESE SAGE

A Siamese sage
sits with his shadow
in the winter sun.
Elegantly furred
in brown and beige
this wise one
occasionally draws
ceremonial claws
from their sheaths of fur.
Ten exquisitely honed
instruments of torture
make his pleasure known.
Flesh is torn from bone
as oriental love
covers us with blood.

Yet must we pour an oblation
of cream to the old one,
we must sit at his paws
beat a small gong
and fill his begging bowl
with fine white rice
for, in our next incarnation
we may be mice.

THE SIAMESE CAT OF THE MONASTERY CONTEMPLATES HIS DEATH AND REINCARNATION.

I sit by the Temple Lake
in the lily shade
where the great golden carp
come gliding through.
I am wise, I am revered
though my coat is frayed -
I am old, my fading eyes
only just blue.
I took the Saffron Path
long long ago
and now the Mouse of Death
gnaws at my heart.

I can stay among you only
till the cold winds blow -
before the dark of winter
I must cast off my shadow -
before the Frangipani
sheds its spring snow.

I cannot be sure
of finding Nirvana
after this death,
There yet may be
a bundle of pale fur
mewling and half blind
left on the bare earth
at the temple door
for a monk to find.

Reincarnate
he will know me again -
when his eyes meet
the blue eyes of the mind
that once was mine.
He will know I came
softly on secret feet
back through the Lotus Gate
to grace his shrine.

THE WINTER COAT

At the Lotus Gate
I sit in the pale light
and meditate
upon my winter coat.
Downy on the belly,
smooth over the shoulders,
It has seal sleeves
and a velvet hood.
Fashioned of Siamese silk
the colour of wild moon
it is softer than any thread
the loom weaves
from a silk cocoon.
It was designer made
aeons ago
by some long gone son
of a snow-leopard
in the fur trade.

The winter will come
to the courtyard
and crystal petals
fall over the temples.
Before the turn of the year
I shall wear my new fur -
a fine robe and so warm
on a winter day
that I can walk through snow
as though it were
a drift of almond blossom
fallen in May.

ON THE DEATH OF A BLUE-POINT SIAMESE

You were the soft blue
incandescence of shadow, evocation
of happiness. For attire
you chose a traditional garment of Thai
silk, and in this incarnation,
wore a brown mask slashed with sapphire.

We watched you at morning, rapt
in the contemplation of Buddha -
or possibly butterflies:
and, strolling at dusk remarked
that the shadow beneath the gardenia
glinted with dragons' eyes.

From behind the dawn a stranger
came, robed in saffron, came with a silver
bell; begging his way -
seeking an idol, he said, for a pagoda -
garden in far Nirvana -
where the silk shadows play.

FESTIVAL OF LIGHTS

A Thai Princess waits for her Siamese Cat
on the River Bank.

I have hung wind-chimes
under the Tulip Trees
by the pagoda
so that the evening breeze
may touch them in passing.
The faint tinkling of silver
will carry my welcome.

Here in another lifetime
you were my shadow
as I followed the willow path
down to the river.
There came a day without sun
and my shadow was gone.

In the tall forest
far away and remote
lies the pavilion
of the Bamboo Flute.
There the lost shadows wait
when the sun has shone.

And you have endured there
till this night when princesses
gather beside the river
to set their fragile lamps
adrift on water -
small lamps, half-flame, half-prayer.

And by their light you will come,
softly with no alarm,
your ears still dipped in the dark,
your belly the colour of moon -
the fur caressing my hand
still wild-silk and warm.

The darkness before moonrise
will tremble with sapphires -
small ghost of the blue eyes
and the intimate paws -
with the sun on the willow path
you were my shadow
now, in the night-time of death
the garden is yours.

THE HOLY CAT
OF
KHOZOUVICTISSA

I climbed to the monastery -
two hundred and fifty stone steps
above the Aegean Sea.
In the marble shadow
I heard a low voice
and saw a pious puss
(Felis Christianus)
in a dark soutane.
Gently he raised a paw
to welcome me.

His eyes were golden as candles
burning before the shrine,
He raised his voice to sing
the Liturgy.

"In kittenhood," he told me,
"I came up in a basket,
long since I took my vows
of sanctity.
I promised never to mouse,
never even to father
a hierarchy."

Now in this sober dress
on silent feet I cross
the sanctuary.
I trust the Patriarch
will declare me a Blessed Puss
after I die.
So that the Toms of the Town
may one day have their own
cat in the sky."

THE SIAMESE ON PATMOS

In the Cyclades the Siamese
are few and far between,
from Nisiros to Amargos
there is hardly a breeding queen.

In the quarter above the harbour
on the old island of Patmos
I met a dark eared stranger.
He said that the fur father
at the head of his line
came over with an old saint
with St. John the Divine
but did not share his vows
of celibacy.
His coat had the soft tint
of the sky before dawn
and though he spoke no Greek
his eyes were blue and deep
as the wine-dark sea.

# CAT OUT OF CONTEXT

For Suli.

A cross-eyed Siamese
with sabre claws
and muffled paws
sits, statue-still
beside our garden urn.
She is ready to leap
on the backs of malefactors
who threaten her temple.

For her the spring air
quivers with incense,
she is listening
to the rustle of saffron robes
as the chanting begins -
'Om mani pedme hum' -
monks in procession come
bringing marigold garlands.

The front door opens -
suddenly her hour
of meditation ends
as trivial chattering
pervades the hall.
We bring no offerings
except a few sardines
from the corner shop.

Perhaps she will decide
to go back to Bankok.

# THE CATS OF KOS

We Byzantine felines
came over from Acre
with the Knights Templar-
We were Ratters Extraordinaire
to the Grand Master
who emblazoned one of us
on a stone shield
in the Crusader castle
on the island of Kos
- Puss Passant on a fur field.

Our eyes were flecked with gold
having looked long
on old icons.
We served St. John
like faithful shadows.

Now our paterfamilias
cat-naps in the shade
under the bougainvillia
while the local mogs
in the tourist trade
work the harbour cafes.
We pad with dirty paws
over the mosaics
(thus breaking the bye-laws).

But it was not like that
in the old days -
In the time when Ali the Cat
(begetter of True Believers)
floated with whiskers down
in the Mandraki harbour
and we held our tails aloft
like the Crusader banners
of holy St. John -
when we fought the good cat fight,
drew claws at the dead of night
for Christendom.

THE CAT OF THE WANLI VASE

White cat of the camelias
in the garden of Shensu
you sip at the stone basin
beside the moon.

You watch the Emperor's carp
in the Lotus Lake -
glissading lemon-gold
and tumbling amber.

You chase the flickering stars
of the firefly candles
that light the painted dusk
of the Dragon Garden.

You crouch by the verandah
of the red pagoda
for you the wind-bells tremble
under the glaze.

THEIR SADNESSES

Subtly the garden is aware of them
the rows of lupins part to let them pass,
the cherry blossom drops its petals when
Their Sadnesses step softly on the grass.

Their ears incline to catch the distant sound
of bells in temple gardens gold with fruit;
they can see lotus blossoms on our pond,
for them the wind picks up a bamboo flute.

They meditate upon the lavender,
on the brief lives of butterflies, upon
a blackbird perching in a conifer
high up until Their Sadnesses have gone.

 A SIAMESE CAT TRIES UNSUCCESSFULLY TO CHANGE THE COURSE OF HISTORY

I came from a country
Eastwards of Eden
to find this garden
and to sit in the shade
of the Paradise Tree
with Eve my Lady.

"My eyes," I told her,
"Are the colour of heaven
and if your gentle hand
should caress my fur
you'll know it softer far
than Adam's hair.

Like a silk shawl
I will lie beside you
through a hundred dawns.
My claws are put away -
there is no harm
in wild-rose thorns.

I will protect you
from the green tree-snake
who speaks with a forked tongue
beside your ear -
for hearts can break that hear
his serpent song."

❄

The Lady Eve walked haughtily away
preferring snake-speak and windfall
Golden Delicious unoriginal sin
and the sweet talk of her sweaty Adam
to bedding with me, soft in my belly-silk...
...heart-sick I took the sad road to Siam.

EMIGRANTS FROM SIAM

We, the blue-eyed Orientals
from the country behind the dawn,
tiptoe in on silk paw -
We come softly as shadows
slipping past the douane
like Siamese thoughts.

We have left the temples
where gongs ding-dong softly,
where our mothers dressed us
in Thai silk, putting the kink
in our tails, where the temple girls -
lovely as lotus flowers,
with almond eyes
and silver finger-nails -
made much of us.
They told us what Confucius
said was a myth,
gave us snakes to play with.

A fur mask of sepia
was formerly 'de rigeur'
but lately the breeding queens
have produced princesses
with lavender ears.
They blame it on the genes.

THE IMMIGRANT PERSIANS

We are the Persian wave
of the Cat People,
we come to colonise
your tortoise-shell shore.
We clutch our pedigrees
and slant our eyes.
We sat on priceless mats
from Shiraz or Tabriz
with the ladies
of the harem at Isfahan.
They fed us sugared mice
and caressed our fur
hour after hour -
having no men.

Once a Sultana
showed us the Peacock Throne -
the emeralds shone
greener than all our eyes
hunting together.
We saw a whisker stir
under a lacquer
screen but in the event
to keep our elegant heads
we had the aplomb
to ignore the rodent.
Now in the courts of Islam
leaner times have come.

We trust that in your country
the eunuchs are friendly
and disposed to proffer
goldfish and rosewater
as we dally at supper
with the ladies of the divan.

Under the veil of night
we will recite
the wise words of Hassan
just under your window
when you are dead tired
and when the moon is up
you should delight
to hear a poet cat
declaim the Rubaiyat
in original Persian.
Morning will find him gone -
like old Khayyam.

THE EMIGRATION OF EGYPTIAN CATS TO BRITAIN

We of Nilotic races
prospered with Rameses
we were all sitting pretty
some of us godesses,
others with laid-back faces -
very like Nerfertiti.
Our effigies in profile,
decorate temple friezes
on the banks of the Nile.
Our elegant ancestors
posed in the fur for sculptors
who carved them in high relief
or cast them in bronze.
(Things the British Museum
would give its eye-teeth
to get its hands on).
Before the cataclysm
We wore enamel ear-rings
to 'Tutankhamuns' -
down the Valley of Kings.
There had to be one of us
in every sarcophagus.
We doubt if our life-style
will compare with the Nile.

THE DORSET TOM

More languourous than lingerie
reclining on a silk settee,
abandoned as a furbelow
cast off in a seraglio
and softer than a Harrods' fur
come from some Arctic neverwhere
with emeralds bought from Tiffany
set where his eyes should really be
our ordinary Dorset Tom
cat-naps in the October sun.

THE MOGGIES

We British Shorthairs
have always lived here.
We came with woad
and Bodicea.
Traditional Ginger Toms
have only one ear.

Men always kicked cats,
put them out at night
although their habitats
were cold and white
with winter snow.
Morale was zero.

Lacking self-esteem
the great Moggy dream
was to work for the devil.
To ride out at owl-hoot
seemed dashingly evil.
On our broomstick handles
we were Hell's Angels.
In our catskin suits
we were Pusses in Boots.

But shortly we found
it was all in the mind
for swiftly our witches
fell into the clutches
of arsonist bishops
too handy with matches.

Broomsticking to the moon
was all hog-wash.
We were treated like trash
being mere menials
sleeping rough in stables,
producing awful quadroon
kittens for someone to drown.

The times were rotten,
no mice ran up clocks -
there was simply the Black Rat -
you took berth as Ship's Cat
or starved on the docks.

In those hard centuries
we had no love.
There were no knees
or laps to sit on
and no Cat Club
of Great Britain.

THE CAT OUTSIDE

For Sed.

I am a pauper cat,
a passing puss
before your door,
I doff my fur cap
and tread a treadmill
with my paw.
I did not eat my fill
since that morsel of mouse
at harvest festival.

I should be welcome
in your house
for every home
deserves a cat
to sit on the mantelpiece
or lie in the fireplace
and occupy the space
in the armchair.

I could cheer up your garden
better than a gnome
and I can make cat-magic
with a chicken bone.

Let me at least
get a paw in the door
for I can smell the roast
of lamb on the stove
so for the love of Mog
spare me a dish.
Remember the furred poor
on a night like this.

THE RICHEST CAT IN THE WORLD

I am a White Persian
with wide nasturtium eyes,
I live in Chelsea
by the riverside
Paul Getty the Second
belongs to me.

I am no area cat
I can never go down
to rat by the Thames
with the toms,
I can never love
a green-eyed Maisie
on the roofs of Chelsea.
If I should venture out
I might not come back -
I fear the Mafia hand
and the man with the sack.
What if a Persian tail
should arrive, gift-wrapped,
with an obscene demand
for millions or more -
followed in every mail
by claw after claw?

I sit by the window
on the safe side
of the glass
while vis-a-vis
the Cockney sparrows
brawl on the grass.
I sometimes wonder if
they envy me.

CATS IN HISTORY

Race Memories of the Wreck of Sir Cloudesley Shovel on the Scilly Islands in 1707.

I am a puss of Lyonesse,
my forebears came ashore
from the King's ships -
press-ganged at Wapping
they swallowed the King's Herring
and went to the war.

Victorious the great fleet sailed
from Spain homeward, but here
there came the shadow of shoals
and on the Gilstone ridges
it foundered and failed -
driven in on a lee shore.

We left with the rats,
sliding down spars and oars
it was every tom for himself
all night in the breakers roar -
and the morning tide
turgid with drowned sailors
and dead ship's-cats.

For years we were poor
we survivors, every last puss
wore a coat stained with tar,
we had no home, no hearth
but only the kelp fire
burning. Seldom a herring
found its way to us.

But now we inherit the earth
and the hungry fish-head days
we knew are long gone.
We stroll on the harbour quay
and loll in the cat-loving warmth
of the lobster-pot sun.

LINES FOR 'TIGGER'

You are young and striped
and newly come
from the tortoiseshell shadow
of the jungle
to make this your home.
You sprawl in your dark
and yellow abandon
under the ceremonial umbrella
of our laburnum.

Your tigers' eyes
reflect the sparrows
but you may think
that birds of paradise
nest in our willows.
You watch the lily-pool
in case the Sika deer
come in the evening cool -
come down to drink.

One of the lesser cats -
you still have the great cat lilt
in your step, the tiger tilt
to your head. You pass
with the same tail-twitch
as did the great Shere Khan
when he went in for the kill
through the jungle grass.

MY POST MODERN CAT

My post-modern cat
has a latch key
she comes and goes
electronically.

She is one of the things
that go flipperty-flap
and bumpity bump
in the night.
Unfortunately
my post-modern cat
is a tramp.

ASTROCATS

We too are made of star-fur, for us
mouse-life is universal.
Nearing the speed of light
we boldly go
through those black Cat-flaps
into time-warped cat-walks -
we need to know
the power of zero gravity
on the flight of sparrows.

Never confuse us
with those bug-eyed, blip-nosed
little green toms
who scramble over the screens
of your Hubble Bubble
earth-tied telescopes.
You must look further out
to the Cat's Eye Nebula
to find us skulking, lynx-like,
in the galaxies.

THE CATS OF BUTLEIGH

Cats
in white spats
lie on ley lines,
and play
'catch as cats can'
with each other.

Cats
in black boots
in cahoots
with their Mistress
the Goddess
and Pan
cannot guess
at the sadness,
the travail,
of man.

Cats
coiled like springs
having flings
after squirrels
and sparrows
must wonder
what harrows
us mortals.

Cats
meditate better
are warmer and safer
on sofas than we are.
They levitate faster
and 'cats-over-matter'
can pre-empt the projects
of witches
in hats.

Cats
so catalytic
can touch us with magic,
philosopher's physic
to make us feel young.
But cats are nomadic
and high-tail it home
by besom-powered flight
in the dark of the night
on the back of a broom
through trees hung
with bats.

THE CAT OF CANDLE LAND

In Candle Land a sonata
flows over the duvet down,
the cadenzas diminish
to heaps of small black notes
that lie still on the floor.
The music springs afresh
and shoals of silver fish
leap up a waterfall -
fall black in silence.

The soft light brushes
the slopes of the duck-down hills
leaving our faces
safely in shadow.
The walls are not listening
to what we say -
to the sweet small-talk
of togetherness.

Touch is an intimate language
and finger tips softer
than half heard sonatas.
Drifting away is gentler
than the moment of falling asleep
that no one remembers.

Then we are wide awake
for an intruder
is pussy-footing softly
through the duvet hills
and a subsidence of down
is threatening the roof
of our retreat.

A soft fur muff
full of delighted breathing
flops on our shoulders.
The Cat of Candle Land
is making sure
we are chaperoned to sleep.

KARIM

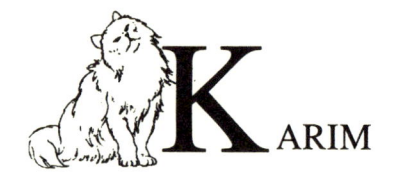

He says he is a Persian Cat,
"Karim"- a name to marvel at

and that his eyes of topaz stone
were looted from the Peacock Throne.

He likes to tell us that he has
just jetted in on a Shiraz

from somewhere east of Isfahan
a rendezvous with old Khayyam?

But we must ask ourselves has he
a crisis of identity?

We are inclined to think his eyes
are mirrors made for butterflies

and that his name is not Karim -
he chose it for the rhyme with 'cream'.

Who was he when he ran away
to find the R.S.P.C.A.?

ON KITCHENER ISLAND

Small cat of a Nile island
your coat is the colour
of sand caressed by shadow.
Your eyes are cabouchons
of chalcedony
flecked tiger-yellow.

You desire fish, alas
I have only piastres.

AT THE NECROPOLIS OF MUMMIFIED CATS

I stand in ritual mourning
in the dry blue air
to honour the furred dead
whose dust lies here.
I think of the anointing
with precious oils, the embalmers -
their funerary gear.

For this one a sarcophagus
scratched with Nile fish,
for that one a mask of sapphire
and a golden bier -
he was appointed 'Cat'
to Queen Hatshepsut.
And on the walls of the tombs
are sealed cat-doors -
about the size of the souls
of the cats of the Nile
in the Thirteenth Dynasty -
who lie with folded paws
waiting eternity.

Luxor 1996

MUSICAL CATS

We were compared to the family of Bachs
for we all put our guts into musicology
though actually we favoured the violin
over the pianoforte.

Perfect pitch resounds from our strings -
for we were martyred for Stradivarius
and his ilk - so sounds like silk
could flow from his Cremona violins.

My grandfather performed (posthumously)
a duet with Yehudi Menuhin -
collaborating in a rendition
of 'Air on a G String'.

THE REVENANTS

Watching them on their cat-walk - their garden wall,
sated with sun - we still ponder the meaning
of their lives beyond the hunting and sleeping
when time runs to that last cat curtain-call.

We still feel their presences when they are gone
when that unwished for journey to the vet
is finally done - or do old cats forget
the glowing logs, the sunlight on the lawn?

Spirits will take the paths they used to live by,
obedient cat-flaps opening as they come
and their cat - shadows crossing a square of sun -
just visible to the believer's eye.

And we will know they go about their business,
though very rarely will cat-silk caress a cheek
the edge will be off the silence, their absences
softened - our nights still soothed and furred with sleep.

THE CAT OF THE TITANIC

I sailed with the Titanic
for the 'Land of the Free'
I carried a sea-cat's ticket
in the name of 'Lucky'.

The milk in my saucer tilted
when the iceberg struck -
I was calm till the rats panicked,
then I pushed my luck.

I swore at the rich poodles,
'stand clear of the falls, you pugs!'
I should have saved my spittle,
they drowned to the last dog.

But I had the guts to survive
that huge commotion
though I lost eight of my lives
in that icy ocean.

They could not tell, in the life-boat,
if it was ME -
or part of an old fur coat
they had pulled from the sea.

THE CATS DEPLORE THE LOSS OF THEIR PROPER PLACE IN THE SCRIPTURES

In the time of King James -
when forefathers were young
and quick of claw -
They summoned the Sages,
Linguists, Givers of Law
to render the Holy Book
in the English tongue.

They gave the beasts their places
in the pages - the birds of the air,
the hart and his hind, the eagles,
the she-wolf, the bear
but they called us the Devil's Disciples,
we were blacker than sin -
they had no room in their Bibles
for the witches' kin.

But we were the watchers for rats
in the Stable straw -
It is writ in the Book of Cats
(of our ancient lore)
that a queen cat came to the crib
with a gift of Fur
while the Word speaks only of Gold,
Frankincense and Myrrh.

When Lazarus lay dead
there was a cat in black
to sit quietly in mourning.
When Martha baked her bread
a cat slept by the stove
and when the Magdalene came
her soft hands understood
our need for love.

In a garden before dawn
there will always be
a cat waiting in shadow
by a dark-leaved tree -
there was just such a fellow
in his cat-skin grey
there at Gethsemane
on Easter Day.

Of all eyes his alone,
- deep green in the gloom -
stared at the moving stone
and saw an unearthly light
shine from the tomb
upon a stranger clad
in radiant white.

Oh dark was the day they took
our race from the Holy Book.

LAST WORDS TO A SIAMESE

This is the parting of ways,
you have come
to the end of the Silk Road
cocooned
in your old robe of shantung
you sit at the door
of your death in the first days
of the spring sun.

Last year your small shadow
fell on the water
where the carp rippled and shone.
In the year to come
white petals will drift over
the old stone pathway
where you sat in the sun.

BREACH OF SECURITY

Precautions are adequate,
I can come to no harm.
There is a burglar alarm
fixed on the outside wall
in an active state.

Then there are those trick locks
on the windows - and in the hall
a spy hole to see that all
visiting hobos will be
deterred. Peculiar keys
ensure security
is fully observed.

Then why do I wake in the night
hearing inaudible feet
coming and going ,
feeling the shadow of silk
almost caressing my cheek -
intangibly blowing?

Is it the substance of grief
shut away long ago
and never allowed to revolt
or come out on parole
as far as I know?

But did I remember to bolt
the cat-door of my soul?

CRUELTY TO ANIMALS

I deprecate the disregard
that people have for cats -
they swing them round, they swing them hard
to measure tiny flats.

They lay their eyes - what a disgrace -
in lines along the road -
Imagine, there's a pussy face
under each lorry's load.

No camel train should thread its way
through any needle's eye -
we must be more humane today
than in the days gone by.

And take your average elephant -
a psychiatric wreck -
because zoologists just can't
let the poor beast forget.

And spineless chaps who bring distress
must somehow understand
its cruel to the ostriches
to stick their heads in sand

I watch them bumbling through the blue
like bangers in the sky
but I condemn the people who
first taught those pigs to fly.

A SUPPLICATION

O Mother, Mary Mother,
what shall I do when I die -
when I go up to heaven
and meet my cats in the sky?

There will be celebrations
when Peter rattles his keys -
with the salaams of Egyptians
and the greetings of Siamese.

Such protestations of Persians
in Oriental furs
and the love-lorn looks of moggies
curled up on the golden chairs.

There will be trouble in heaven
with green-eyed jealousy
and angel-feathers flying -
all for the love of me.

There will be Burmese daggers
to carve an ear or two
and Siamese with flick-knives
(and eyes of Virgin blue).

O Mother, Mary Mother,
I fear the fur will fly
at the great cat fight in heaven
when I meet my cats in the sky.

HAIKU

At the Last Supper
the cat under the table
ate the broken bread

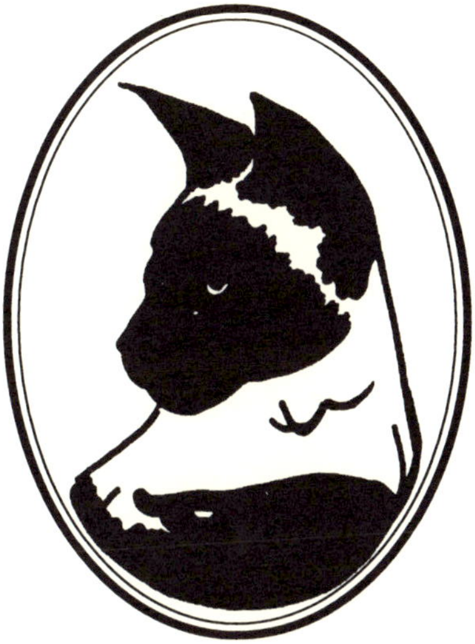